TIK TOK MARKETING

FOR

ENTERPRENEURS

The Beginner's Guide to Grow Your Business with Tik Tok and Influencers Marketing

Robert Kasey

All rights to this book are reserved. No permission is given for any part of this book to be reproduced, transmitted in any form or means, electronic or mechanical, stored in a retrieval system, photocopied, recorded, scanned, or otherwise. Any of these actions requires the proper written permission of the publisher.

All Rights Reserved

Copyright © 2021

Robert Kasey

Disclaimer

All erudition contained in this book is given for informational and educational purposes only. The author is not in any way accountable for any result or outcome that emanate from using this material. Constructive attempts have been made to provide information that is both accurate and effective, but the author is not bound for the accuracy or use/misuse of this information.

TABLE OF CONTENTS

INTRODUCTION 6

CHAPTER ONE 11
    What is Tik Tok? 11

CHAPTER TWO 25
    Why is Tik Tok is Valuable Platform for Brands and Influencers? 25

CHAPTER THREE 41
    Finding Your Target Tik Tok Audience 41

CHAPTER FOUR 58
    Strategy on Building Tik Tok Content 58

CHAPTER FIVE 72
    Why Is Tik Tok's Algorithm Key in the Success of Marketing and E-Commerce? 72

CHAPTER SIX 92
    Entrepreneurs on Tik Tok 92

CHAPTER SEVEN 103
    Understanding Hashtags and Hashtag Challenges 103

CHAPTER EIGHT 118
    Running an Influencer Marketing Campaign 118

CHAPTER NINE 139

Uncertainties and Certainties of Social Media As Regards To Business 139

CONCLUSION 159

INTRODUCTION

After the exit of the Vine application, Musical.ly and Tik Tok merged to make the fastest-growing short-form video application. Tik Tok, owned by Bytedance bought musical.ly for $1 billion; today, Tik Tok is the world's number one for short-form video content creation and utilization. Therefore, it is named the world's most valuable startup, $75billion. Tik Tok is the newest trend in social media, with over 2 billion downloads on the App Store and Google Play globally.

It has been downloaded more than 80 million times in the United States and has over 800 million active users monthly. The largest demographic of Tik Tok users is between 16 and 24. The platform consists of 15- and 60-second video recorded by the user that rely on in-application editing functions in combination with the other significant social players. Since its birth in 2018, Tik Tok has developed from a video-creation application exclusively meant for users to communicate their creativity to a marketing and advertising haven.

The beauty of Tik Tok is that anybody can open an account and quickly begin making content and acquire attention from the users. To make it simple, this is how the Tik Tok artificial intelligence or algorithm works. The application has witnessed fast development since the fusion with Musical.ly, and a portion of this development is because of an aggressive promoting procedure or marketing strategy by the organization.

At this moment, Tik Tok's algorithm is genuinely easy to comprehend. It is easy to build upon, which could suggest why numerous creators, entrepreneurs, and individuals are directing their attention toward Tik Tok. The capability of growth for business on Tik Tok is remarkable.

Getting acquainted with Tik Tok and producing your content might prompt a ton of business growth and be an extraordinary advertising strategy for a brand. There are two ways for the Tik Tok advertising technique: working with influencers or creating original and unique content. Each one of these techniques has its advantages and time commitments.

Influencer marketing at its heart looks like storytelling and with enough adaptability to tell their story to their followers to promote and recommend a brand's products and services. Additionally, businesses can use their account to run advertisements and promotions, thereby moving their range to be more global and to younger people in the process.

Lately, Tik Tok launched a native analytics tool for Pro accounts, which are like Instagram creator accounts. Tik Tok's analytics dashboard collects information about your general audience and the performance of published content. Likewise, they propelled another feature that permits few users to include a link in their bio. This link can help businesses to direct quickly and effectively their customers and other users to their sites from the app, thereby achieving their shopping goals.

CHAPTER ONE
What is Tik Tok?

THE RELEVANCE OF TIK TOK IN THE BUSINESS WORLD

Tik Tok is the newest trend in social media, with more than 2 billion downloads on the App Store and Google Play and over 800 million active users. The platform comprises 15- to 60-second user recorded videos that allow in-application editing and integration with the other significant social players. The biggest demographic of Tik Tok users are between 16 and 24. Since its inception, Tik Tok has developed from a video-creation application exclusively meant for users to communicate their creativity to a marketing and advertising haven.

Over the last year, brands have created accounts on the platform to explore and connect with customers. On Tik Tok, you can find everybody from influencers and celebrities to legislators and common people. The appeal of Tik Tok for organizations is the sheer number of active users on the platform. It's still unclear how the algorithm works precisely, but it is, by all means, a lot simpler for video content to become a web trend on Tik Tok than on other social platforms.

Tik Tok has different unique effects and features to add to your video, including music. Users usually make lip-sync videos in the style of Musical.ly, where they spell the words of well-known songs. In a way, it resembles making your music video. Tik

Tok has pretty much every well-known song on the radio accessible without copyright infringement issues.

Tik Tok is an application for iOS and Android where users can make and share 15-second videos. It works like most social applications with followers who like and comment content. Hashtags let users find content by theme. On paper, Tik Tok doesn't sound different from most applications; however, it is a great deal of fun and has some intriguing content. Lip-synching videos are accessible, yet so are short videos of band promotion, enchanting stunts, and various tricks. Probably the best feature of Tik Tok is its editing options, giving users assets to make fun videos. It gives them intriguing features, for example, the possibility to record their reaction to a video while they're watching it. Users can likewise record their very own video utilizing the sound from another video.

Tik Tok was launched in China in 2016 under the name "Douyin" by a Chinese firm named Bytedance established in 2012 by Zhang Yiming; Tik Tok is a video-driven social media platform or a short-video sharing platform. It was rebranded as Tik Tok for a global market a year later. Today, it's one of the fastest-growing applications available, ranking as the third best free app in the Apple Store of free downloads in the Apple Store. Its parent company, ByteDance, merged Tik Tok with the mainstream Musical.ly application to acquire a more extensive user base. The Tik Tok name was kept.

However, the entirety of Musical.ly's content was brought into Tik Tok.

Tik Tok bought the prevalent music-focused application Musical.ly for about $1billion, taking on it's entertaining, casual, heavy-lip-sync content style and snowballing the social platform's popularity. By 2018, Tik Tok surpassed all other social applications, including Instagram, with over 100 million downloads. The application has been downloaded worldwide more than 2 billion times and has been elected the world's most valuable startup at $75billion US. Its reach and scope are tremendous, as the application is hugely prominent in 150 markets and 75 languages globally. Its average user spends about an hour on the app every day, Tik Tok represents the rise of the video-sharing apps.

In the early years of its existence, Tik Tok slid under the vast majority's radar. Still, in 2020, one can no longer overlook the influence it has had around the world or the opportunities it has created for individuals, brands, and businesses. Due to these unprecedented times we are all living through, engagement on social media has increased radically, and more people are exploring the new platforms. Tik Tok is at the forefront of those platforms; Tik Tok has started to compete with Instagram in popularity, and this is something that the digital landscape is continually reminding

Tik Tok shares some aesthetic and functional similarities with Snapchat and

Instagram, but it has its core characteristics as well; Tik Tok turned over the midpoint between the familiar self-coordinated and experience-based feed on algorithmic observation and inference. Tik Tok employs artificial intelligence to analyze users' interests and preferences through their interactions with the content. With other results obtained by the algorithms of other services utilized by the user (e.g. YouTube and Netflix) with a list of recommended videos. TikTok interprets the user's individual preferences and provides content that they would enjoy. One can become famous and make money through Tik Tok.

As the platform Tik Tok continues to surge in fame, numerous brands are thinking about how this platform is shaping culture and relevant discussions. They want to get in on the opportunity to increase their brand's impact. Many new updates are on the horizon for Tik Tok in 2020. Tik Tok is one of the fastest-growing platforms; TikTok is ahead of other popular platforms such as LinkedIn, Snapchat, Pinterest, and Twitter by the number of active users of about 800million. By comparison, it took Instagram six years before it had the number of active users that Tik Tok has. With such a fast growth rate, there are unlimited opportunities for brands to activate influencer marketing campaigns on Tik Tok.

Tik Tok can make someone become an influencer who helps brands and organizations to promote their products and services for a charge. Tik Tok is a go-to application for short-form mobile video with a sole mission: to inspire creativity and network, and to connect users with people around the world while offering satisfaction. It ultimately wants to build a worldwide community where users can make and share their life spontaneously and discover the world around them.

It is an inclusive application built upon the foundation of creative expression. Tik Tok urges users to celebrate what makes them extraordinary while finding a community that does likewise. Tik Tok Is aware and take into account that its users originate from a vast expansiveness of nationalities and societies. It considers the social norms and local guidelines of the countries it operates in.

Nowadays, applications have helped numerous businesses reach their target customers and future markets; looking from one point of view, one would prefer promoting on various channels to attract required and relevant customers. Social media and influencers are becoming a staple of marketing. Ever-increasing numbers of marketers recognize influencer marketing as an effective marketing strategy; however, with the plethora of social platforms to choose from, it's difficult to tell which ones to target.

Alongside this increasing dependence on social media within marketing, comes the rise of social media user fatigue, a perceived propensity of users to feel the need to 'step back' from social media after becoming overwhelmed by the choices of different platforms and the pressure of keeping followers. The truth is, people are getting bored and tired of the negative aspects of increasing established social media platforms. Many are now looking for a new, native-edited space to express themselves, share content, and connect with other like-minded individuals. This is where Tik Tok kicks in.

Tik Tok is a platform that seems to value out of the box creativity, with the option to use filters, augmented reality features, music clips and even dialogue from TV shows and movies to edit together a short 15-second video clip quickly. Tik Tok is a social media mobile app with a large community of users centered on video content. Tik Tok users film short videos and edit them with effects, filters, captions, and music, then post them for their Tik Tok followers. Content creators use hashtags and identify which popular category they fit into to be discovered by non-followers more easily.

Much of the app content is humorous. Some of the most popular genres include short skits, lip-synching, cringe videos, and so on. One of the most popular phenomena is the inundation of "challenges" posted across the platform that creates a ripple effect as everybody contributes with their version.

In addition to direct ads, many brands are using Tik Tok's superstar influencers to support their brand campaigns and reaching millions of users in the process. Tik Tok is generally well-known among people between 16 and 24, making up 41% of the total user-base. Asides age, the other stats about Tik Tok is the reasonably even popularity across the board. 56% of Tik Tok users are male, and 44% are female. The app is available in 150 markets in 75 languages, and iPhone or Android usage is a 52%/47% split. As long as you're in the correct age range, you can probably find your customers.

Considering that, it is recommended to possibly use Tik Tok for marketing if you have a young audience. While there's no doubt that older people will begin to use the platform soon, brand marketing resources will probably be better spent elsewhere if that's your targeted audience.

CHAPTER TWO

Why is Tik Tok is Valuable Platform for Brands and Influencers?

Is it Relevant in the Entrepreneurial World?

Tik Tok has around 800 million active users, which is more significant than Twitter and Pinterest taken together. With this muzzle blast of new content to devour, its hooking power has gotten clear. Tik Tok is probably not going to be a fad. This may seem like a marketing goldmine, mainly because there might be less rivalry while different businesses dither to get aboard. However, engaging in with prospective customers in a place where they go to be entertained requires a nuanced, cautious approach.

Tik Tok advertising and marketing is a significant part of the 21st-century social media marketing strategy. The act of selling and promoting products and services has moved beyond the usual selling in stores and malls or advertising on mass media to social media. This has helped brands and influencers target their customers or the types of people they hope will become their customers.

There are two options for Tik Tok marketing strategy: working with influencers or creating unique and original content. Each of these strategies has its benefits and time commitments; Influencer marketing helps in concentrating on the individuals to whom appeal and to impact target costumers' behavior. If a brand sells to young people, they could consider working with influencers on Tik Tok. Like YouTube and other social media applications, Tik Tok's most crucial component is sharing videos. Any Tik Tok influencer marketing campaign will spin around influencers making, sharing, and once in a while live streaming videos that will promote a brand and make it alluring to their followers. The more engaging the videos, the better they reverberate with the audience.

Influencer marketing at its heart resembles storytelling. The most horrible mistake on Tik Tok would be to post anything looking like a traditional advertisement or trying to give an influencer specific guidelines. A brand needs to give their influencers enough flexibility to tell their story to their followers to keep them authentic. The influencers' followers will instantly know whether the videos promote brand products or not. If the videos are made in a different style from the influencer's typical videos, their followers will react badly.

Why You Should Use Tik Tok for Influencer Marketing

As with all influencer marketing, the way to have success on Tik Tok is working with influencers whose followers are linked with your target market. For this reason, for influencer promoting and marketing to be productive and successful for brands and businesses on Tik Tok, you have to interest the Tik Tok demographic because Tik Tok's youthful demographic finds traditional ads disdainful.

These influencers have audiences that might want to purchase your products, so for a piece of your marketing budget, you can partner with them and make an influencer marketing campaign. Pay these influencers to utilize your products on-camera or otherwise promote your product in their videos, and you'll get your products before new eyes. But more significantly, you will earn some of your customers' trust as well. One of every three customers trust an influencer's opinion more than a brand, so utilize that for your potential benefit.

Brands simply need to work with their influencers to think to creative strategies that help them arouse the curiosity of their audience and to build enthusiasm for their brand and product. Similar to much influencer marketing, brands can take most notification of measurements (statistics) relating to commitment and awareness. These can be a brilliant guide for brand loyalty.

The benefit of looking for well-known influencers in your specialty on Tik Tok is that they will have a vast user base who will pay attention to any video that they share talking about your brand/product.

Always take note, relevance is a higher priority than reach. Don't just decide on

Tik Tok influencers with the most massive followings. Go for those with the most appropriate audience for your goals; the golden rule of Influencer Marketing is that relevance is more important than reach. When you have chosen suitable influencers, you should get in touch with them and structure a partnership. You need to guarantee that any deal is adequate for your influencers. They will not want any involvement except if there is something for them, and they can perceive how it can support their followers.

Don't just move toward the individuals behind accounts with the most massive followings. It will not only be unbelievably expensive to work with them, but they could fail in promoting your brand or products; however, numerous references to your product and brands could fail to be noticed. Search for those who are posting popular videos in your specialty by exploring the discover tab. Look through a bunch of keywords that identify with your industry, products, or services. Take note of the users with most followers or mainstream videos within this topic, watch their post to decide if they suit your product for your product, and consider connecting with them.

Likewise, marketing can be done without using influencers on Tik Tok. It has taken a while for Tik Tok to implement it. However, there is now a formal advertising system. Brands can also promote their business by using a business Tik Tok account. However, just like any other social network, it can be tough to build a sizeable audience on Tik Tok. This is so especially for businesses that don't have a staff of a similar demographic as their audience and struggle to run a business account. It is far easier for most brands to work with Tik Tok's established broadcasters or their influencers than to build a cherished and much-followed business account.

Making your content can be a powerful, marketing strategy. However, it will take a lot of of time, creativity, and resources. Tik Tok is largely dependent to viral content, so your content must be viral as well, otherwise, it will probably be overlooked by Tik Tokers.

The least demanding, best approach to ensure that your original content becomes mainstream and shareable is to dive into the "trend" culture. Use the find page to follow trending hashtags, and afterward create your version of the trend that includes a component of your business. Bonus points if it's funny or entertaining to increase your chance of virality.

Another easy way to create accessible content is to offer how-to's, tips and tricks, or insider secrets from your industry. If you own a bakery, you can show a pared-down, visually appealing version of the steps in a recipe, such as baking a cake to the tune of a pop song where the final version appears when you show yourself snapping your fingers. This method is a doubly effective strategy in the wake of the COVID-19 pandemic, where numerous in-person services have been compelled to figure out how to offer something different online. Create a Tik Tok of your top yoga models for stress relief or how to create extravagant cocktails in your kitchen to keep your content relevant to your audience while they stay home.

When you have created a content using one of these ideas or an original one you came up with for your business, add a couple of consistent, relevant hashtags to your post before you upload it since this is how users who do not follow you will find it.

Brands can also make a marketing campaign on Tik Tok using Paid Ads: Tik

Tok has recently introduced this possibility. It is still early to see how successful or cost-effective these will be, especially when targeting the advertising-hating millennial demographic. Tik Tok has proposed that brands combine the use of one of the following ad formats:

1. Brand Takeover: These ads appear in the user's feed before they see any other user content. They're linkable to the advertiser's landing page and are exclusive to different categories. Mostly, just one ad can show in that space for a particular category each day.

2. In-Feed Native Videos: regardless of whether brands use them as a paid ad or their company Tik Tok channel, they could consider sharing some in-feed native videos. These can last up to 15 seconds, although they can share brief video clips as short as nine seconds.

3. Hashtag Challenges: Tik Tok users respond exceptionally well to challenges. There are usually multiple challenges going on at any time for Tik Tok users to participate. The usual type of Tik Tok challenges involves somebody setting a challenge (beginning it with a hashtag), hence the Hashtag Challenge. The challenge typically challenges others on Tik Tok to make and share a particular type of video.

4. Branded Lenses: Branded lenses are like the Snapchat 2D and 3D lenses for faces and photos.

Re-posting videos that were created on Tik Tok in other social media platforms like Instagram and Twitter is a hugely popular practice. If businesses have an engaged audience on those other platforms, they can likewise take advantage of the Tik Tok editing tools to create video content for their followers.

Why Tik Tok is a Valuable Platform for Brands?

Tik Tok is relatively new and has exploded in popularity. With Tik Tok on the rise, it is natural that companies are eager to examine and utilize the platform to connect with hard-to-reach but incredibly valuable potential customers. Simultaneously, it is imperative to combine experimentation with an excellent content strategy to make a decent digital first impression with platform users.

Tik Tok is experiencing a period of exponential growth at the moment, which implies that there is a broad audience ready to be taken advantage of by creative and fast-thinking brands. Brands who have effectively tuned to Tik Tok early have received tremendous benefits in term of brand impact, often with very little investment.

Brands must position themselves as a creative force to be reckoned with and possibly shift their reach to another, more global, and younger user base. Besides, it is relatively easy to achieve a viral status on Tik Tok. Unlike Instagram or YouTube, even accounts with zero followers can get millions of views on a new video. Content truly is king on Tik Tok.

With the huge potential for brand impact and reach, Tik Tok could soon be making it much easier to redirect the traffic from the platform by introducing a link in bio. This means businesses can now drive traffic to their websites from the app and direct followers to shopping destinations. Only a few users can currently add a link to their Tik Tok bio, but it is well possible that this possibility will be spread in oncoming months.

And for the time being, all users can add links to their Instagram and YouTube profiles from their Tik Tok profile.

CHAPTER THREE
Finding Your Target Tik Tok Audience

According to the famous entrepreneur Richard Branson, "Business opportunities are like buses; there is always another one coming." You may have missed the grand opening of Instagram, or the chance to be one of the few first influencers. It is never too late. If you wish to still make it on the most recent trending social media platform, Tik Tok is another opportunity.

Tik Tok may seem pretty much new and have not yet gained a worldwide audience. But contrary to what you may be thinking, influence on this platform is a must to reach a wider audience. It is reported that this platform, like Facebook, Twitter, and Instagram, has a very high percentage of mostly teens and young adult users. And just like any other platform, the user base must define your target audience and your influence on them.

This is necessary because the influence on any social media platform involves gathering several followings and likes. And followers and likes come when the product you're offering suits them. Many people target just anybody in a bid to get fans forcefully, but they may not end up going anywhere, because they are dealing with the wrong audience. Imagine being a law student, and then someone comes to advertise spare parts of an airplane. You have nothing to do with that, even if you fly on a plane. Plane maintenance is someone else's job.

The right audience is as crucial. Chris Guillebeau, in his book, "The $100 Start-Up", gives two ways to gather the target audience. These are:

1. Traditional demographics of the users which involves their ethnicity, Sex/Gender, Income, Location, and Age.

2. New Demographics which consists of their interests, Passions, Skills, Beliefs, and Values.

Millionaire Entrepreneurs

It is great to have fans on social media, but as an entrepreneur, you need to have an engaged following; people who will be loyal not just to you but to the product you offer. Some entrepreneurs connect their website to their Tik Tok accounts, so people get automatically redirected.

Other entrepreneurs have found the secrets to reach a lot of people on Tik Tok, by creating compelling videos of their luxurious lives, and probably at the end of the video they will tell people they will teach them how to make money so that they can be followed. They have huge fan bases even if they never come to eventually telling them how to make money.

Making money may not be as easy as these people figure it to be, but our Generation Z is never a fan of the rigorous process to achieve great wealth. This is why internet frauds are on the rise every day. Therefore, uploading a video teaching 16 – 23 years old (mostly on Tik Tok), the rigorous steps you took to become a millionaire are generally useless, which is why millionaire entrepreneurs do this.

Taking a Cue from Other Social Media Platforms

Attractiveness

On Tik Tok, your product has to be saleable to people in a precise age range, and you have to be compelling enough through your videos so they can buy it. Ksenia Zaharova, writes in, "How to Sell on Instagram," that 67% of Instagram users consider clear, detailed images to be even more important than the product description. Therefore, if these quality posts have links to to the site where they they can buy the product, they are likely to make impulsive buying decisions for your product.

Demographics

As stated above, taking note of the target audience by knowing who they are, what they are like, what they want, and how they want it is crucial in selling your products. From studies, it is estimated that 90% of Americans make purchase by impulse, which amounts to $200 of extra charges each month. Using these facts will move you toward the right product prices for single products.

If your target is young urban female or male, the right marketing approach will get them buying, if you know their behaviors.

A buyer persona is an example of tool entrepreneurs can use to know the audience. It could be written in an Excel document and it consists of information like:

- What age range do you reach?
- What's your average customer's level of income?
- What is their typical value?
- What their common pinpoint?
- What's the solution?
- Which type of content works best?

Surveys like this could also tell an entrepreneur about the kind of products their target audience wants. It could range from this to asking simple questions like;

- What is the audience's most significant problem with buying products like yours?
- What is the foremost question they may have about the product?
- How can you help to solve the problem?

The survey above was suggested in Chris Guillebeau's book.

Trends

It is wise for entrepreneurs to make good advantage of trending campaigns, mostly in the form of hashtags. Using the right hashtags at the right moments brings the right customers. There will be details on using hashtags to increase your influence in subsequent chapters. The description on your page tells whether customers will like you for who you are or dislike you for who you are not. Make the best use of the description part when filling in your information on Tik Tok. The description should be specific and detailed, including a few notes about what you sell, shop policies, and possibly about who you are and the hashtag of your accont. The audience will be motivated to follow you if they know you have them at heart and show it. Your description could be the start of a beautiful, fruitful relationship with them.

Collaborate with Other Entrepreneurs

Collaborating with competitors, people who are where you want to be, or people who have products that are doing well could expose you to their audience and bring you to advertise your product well. Customers are usually loyal to brands they trust, and if these brands happen to be endorsing you, then it's a win.

Staying Active

"Being pro-active" is the word. Your willingness to actively engage in discussions goes a long way in increasing your influence on Tik Tok. Follow other entrepreneurs, like their posts and comment. People want to see that you are who you say you are. If there is a current trending movement or happening, give your input on it whether it's some children dying of hunger somewhere in the world, or the Black Lives Matter movement. Show that you are part of it and that you care.

Connect Other Platforms

Facebook, Instagram, and Twitter, where other Zoomers are active, are platforms On which to be active, too, as an entrepreneur. Many will like to check you up on other social media platforms to see if they find you. You have to present the same image. As a busy entrepreneur, it may seem difficult to handle all these, but applications such as Tik Tok help you schedule posts for many days ahead.

Other platforms like Facebook also helps to connect to specific niches, which is a big win for your business.

How Business-Minded People Can Take Advantage of Tik Tok

An entrepreneur is business-minded; that is why there is something like an "Entrepreneurial Mindset." Even if there's no physical product, an entrepreneur will always find a way to do business. And if there is no product, affiliate marketing could be the catch. Mustafa Mohammed and Jide Maduako's story is one example of innovation with an entrepreneurial mindset. These two, one a business economist and the other a Computer scientist, developed an application that helps influencers make money through affiliate marketing. And with the increase of Tik Tok influence during the COVID-19 outbreak, their income increased more than ever in some months. As of July 7, 2020, Yoke Network has over 2000 influencers and over 600 million total audience.

Highlighted below are the different ways business-minded people can do business through Tik Tok.

1. Personal Products

Do you have a fashion shop, Artwork, or any other product you will sell? Social platforms such as Tik Tok should not be viewed as distractions. An entrepreneur should see opportunities in most places, which is how you must see Tik Tok. Having over 1000 followers on Tik Tok makes you eligible to go live. This will increase your viewership, and fans can gift money.

2. Affiliate Sales

In the absence of one's product, it is possible to sell other products and earn a commission. This is called Affiliate Marketing. A lot of influencers are doing this now. Also, more brands are more conscious of this now and probably get more buyers online than offline. These brands sponsor your videos on Tik Tok if you are an affiliate marketer for them. The figure from this could range from $10,000 and above for over 7 million fans. Keep in mind that the more fans one has, the more influence over their spending habit one can exert.

3. Other Products Related to the Application

Like the two entrepreneurs mentioned above, Mustafa and Jide, one can develop products that can be linked to Tik Tok. One beautiful thing about this is that, as Tik Tok grows, the product grows too. For Instagram, as the number of users increases, the number of users using tools like Instagram, Iconosquare, and Latergram increases.

4. Teach People How to be Successful Entrepreneurs on Tik Tok

This is another way an entrepreneur can make money from the platform. Like this book you are reading; one can make videos about how to utilize every feature on the app or any other thing. Answering people's questions is solving a problem, and filling a need, which is what entrepreneurs are specialized in.

CHAPTER FOUR

Strategy on Building Tik Tok Content

Tik Tok's extraordinarily creative and user-friendly algorithm makes it a winning social media platform. It enables anyone to open an account, create content, and gain attention.

Tik Tok videos are a great place to showcase your business and what you plan to offer. If your product requires assembling, you can create user-friendly, step by step videos that can be linked to your packaging. If you just want a full display of the business behind the scene shots, you can create that. And if you just want to express yourself yourself, Tik Tok has provided options for that, as well.

It is an excellent platform for fun and work, but what matters is reaching out to other users. It is how content can be created and presented to appeal and pass over the message they carry.

1. Creativity: The most significant selling point on any social media is creativity when delivering the content. Be ready to invest your time and other resources available in building up your content to be user-friendly and appealing. Several options enable creativity on the platform. Creativity is endless, and all it requires are some thoughts on unique and likable content.

You can include utilizing Tik Tok effects on your post. Tik Tok offers a wide range of effects to help to help your content to stand out.

2. Concept: Normally, Tik Tok videos are regarded as a particular concept. A search will give you options for trending concepts that you can incorporate into your content. This is also useful for brands and businesses as they get across to their target audience through this.

3. Profile: Like other social media channels, your profile description indicates what type of content your audience can expect from you. That is why you need to be unique but still clearly communicate who you are and what you deliver.

This also includes your profile picture. Use a profile picture that is clear, unique, and outstanding. And if you are using a video instead, as Tik Tok made it possible, bring your creativity into the mix.

3. Hashtag Challenges: Hashtags are used in many other social platforms for searching and sorting content. The same applies to Tik Tok. A specific hashtag is used for a challenge as part of a viral trend, as an encouragement for users to participate in making similar videos.

The idea is to make the content fun, easy, and meaningful. Brands have made use of this hashtag challenges to promote themselves on the platform successfully.

4. **Make Exciting Videos that are Consistent with the Message You**

Want to Pass Over: Tik Tok videos can last as long as one minute, giving you sixty seconds to express yourself and the message you want to pass over. Make them count. And as mentioned earlier, be sure to use creativity.

Tips for Effective Tik Tok Marketing

If the target for your brand or business includes anyone within the age of 13 to 30, Tik Tok marketing will get you the desired audience, target customers, and future markets. Tik Tok has over one billion users and growing. Its developing range of ad options makes it a prospective platform for marketers to promote their products.

Here is some information you should consider to gain success in marketing your brand or on this growing platform.

1. Consider the type of market you want to reach: Tik Tok major users are the generation Z and generation X. But we can say that it reaches out to the Millennials as well. If you expect your market audience to be within this range, you should go right ahead.

The good news is that Tik Tok promises to become a social media app that will be everybody's favorite. So this is the time to build your brand and business on this platform.

2. If you are sure you want to make your Tik Tok account mainly business-related, you need to change it to a pro-account: This will enable you to track your analytics and overall growth. You will be able to see how your videos are doing and how much response your content is getting back.

It is just like the analytics you have on Instagram, but here you have Tik Tok analytics.

3. Be sure to follow current Tik Tok trends: When you see people use a hashtag on the discovery page or see a topic that shows up a lot on your "For You" page, you should know that it is what is trending at that time. Tik Tok trends can be powerful and useful in gaining attention to your brand or business.

Your creativity helps in making those trends work for you and how you can fit those trends around your business. Following prominent content creators to ensure you stay up to trend could work in scoring numerous interest points. A lot of trends are rapidly going viral, and immediately reacting to these trends gives higher chances to your video to go viral, too.

These trends may vary, from contents to hashtag and challenges. And they can be fast-moving. So be ready to keep up with the craze.

4. Make use of suitable hashtags: Making use of hashtags that are popular and people are interested in could bring your brand or business into the spotlight. Like every other social media platform, hashtags help categorize and sort out topics and contents to make them easy to find. Using the most relevant hashtags will prompt engagement on your content.

Hashtags can be measured with insights such as clicks, number of views, engagement, and trending slots. So when deciding on hashtags to use, look up for the ones you think will fit your content and make use of of hashtags which are slightly less use. This is because your content could get swamped in a sea of content. That might nullify the effect of visibility And make you invisible to those who are most relevant to your campaign.

Using hashtags will get you more followers, help enhance the range of your content, and identify competitors.

5. Create hashtag challenges: This is a significant way to promote brands and events. Like Jimmy Fallon, celebrities that started the hashtag "tumbleweed challenge" and business houses like McDonalds, which ran #bigmactiktok challenge, have gathered millions of views.

The hashtag challenge campaigns are usually non-sponsored. All you need are ideas of challenges that are easy to do and fun, that will pass over the message you want. Hashtag challenges by influencers are positive for extensive reach, and you can make use of that to spread your brand message.

6. **Utilizing influencer marketing:** Using Tik Tok influencers is a great use to generate content for your own Tik Tok profile and get a response to your products from influencers' followers. They enable you to present your content to the world by building a reputation for the quality of the content they share on your behalf. Being in a productive work relationship with people who can influence your potential customers increases your chances of visibility on the platform.

7. **Post often, comment regularly and encourage comments on your post:** Just like most social networks, your followers appreciate regular content on your account. You can say that the more content you post, the simpler it will be for

people to find your account and decide to follow you.

Also, taking the time to look at other people's content and making meaningful comments will build meaningful conversations with potential customers.

8. Let your contents have a theme: Your business offers a particular or specific product, and that should be the basis for your content creation. Specificity gives you a consistent image. And building this consistency over time will help you gain a following of people interested in what you have to offer.

You want your content to pass over a message and be visually appealing, so a theme would give it a personality at the eyes of your audience.

9. Make use of Tik Tok campaign options: Tik Tok's formal advertising system can be utilized to make your product well-known. There are three types of such ads available.

1. In-feed native ads: This is very similar to Instagram stories in full-screen mode. These are skippable ads and have the option of adding website links and "Order Now" buttons that enable users to land on your page directly.

2. Hash-tag challenges ads: In this type of advertising, a user is served a banner ad that is put up on the discover page depending on the user content that takes the user to a page of instructions of the featuring challenge. This tool targets a specific audience and can be measured with banner views, clicks, number of user-generated content, number of views, trending slots, and engagement.

3. Brand takeover ads: This form of advertising uses a mix of images, short video clips, and GIF's that link to a landing page or the hostage challenge of any set. This ad makes use of a category, and only a single brand can take up a specific category per day.

Although Tik Tok still has a long way to go, it shows great potential to become a lasting social media platform. But with the surge in the number of users, promoting your brand and business on this platform would get you your desired audience.

CHAPTER FIVE
Why Is Tik Tok's Algorithm Key in the Success of Marketing and E-Commerce?

Tik Tok has carved a name for itself in the crowded social space, turning into a global phenomenon. From comedy videos to lip-synch, from cooking tutorials to do-it-yourself home design, dance videos, and the sky is the limit from there. Tik Tok genuinely makes us feel like we can do everything. There is nothing worse than the feeling of posting one's most recent, perfect work only to wake up the next morning and see little or no views and likes. That is colossal disappointment; to avoid this, the Tik Tok algorithm helps videos receive the sort of affection and attention they deserve. Some factors, like user interactions, video information, and device and account settings along with Tik Tok's algorithm, decide how well video performs.

How Does Tik Tok's Algorithm Work?

Tik Tok algorithm is not as basic as those of some other social platforms out there, yet that does not mean there are no strategies to improve your reach and engagement because some factors influence your video's prosperity. The first, and ostensibly most significant, idea to understand is how Tik Tok feeds your content to its users. An essential way to understand Tik Tok's algorithm is by separating it into two areas:

First, Tik Tok gets a video and releases an initial push to viewers. When this is done, the algorithm gives your video a performance rating. This includes how many shares, comments, and likes your video gets during its initial release. At this point, the algorithm compares the number of view of the video with the like it gets, setting off the platform to show the video to more people.

Your Tik Tok feed is ultimately divided into two parts, your "Following" and the "For You" page. While the "Following" page may let you see what your friends are doing, the "For You" page is a useful tool to build your visibility and possible fluctuation. This is an excellent and ideal time to note that Tik Tok not exclusively drives you to fame, it can likewise be an incredible marketing tool. The constant stream of edited content is not just addicting, but exceptionally boosted to posts from users, creators, and businesses alike, that you interact with.

As indicated by the Tik Tok Algorithm, the "For You" page is the initial phase in winning the Tik Tok lottery. With a better understanding of how Tik Tok algorithm works, it is much easier for users to gain popularity with a potential user reach of more than 1 billion people. Tik Tok fame isn't unreasonably out of reach, and with viral content creation that is pertinent, trending, and engaging, the popularity is around the corner.

As a new user, Tik Tok Algorithm shows you the "For You" page as the first thing you see when you open the application, containing unlimited videos that you could like; as the user keeps utilizing Tik Tok, their "For You" page mirrors the user's preferences. The system suggests content by ranking videos based on a combination of factors, beginning from interests the user expresses as a new user and changing things s/he shows they are not intrigued by and this is the reason why Tik Tok is a triumph. It's not social media, it's social entertainment. Likewise, another primary explanation behind its prosperity is that it hits your sweet spot suggesting you suggesting you content posted by your friends/people you follow.

Tik Tok is utilizing AI to assess the quality of each shared video. Everybody understands that content is king, which applies to Tik Tok; great content equals social achievement. At the point when a video is uploaded, Tik Tok shows it to few users in popular trending videos. This way, the user doesn't get bored. The algorithm, at that point, assess the statics of your video, such as the number of likes, comments, and shares it gets. It is the viral videos that eventually act as the carrot on the stick, hooking users to watch to an ever-increasing number of videos.

The rate of likes brands and users should aim to is one for every ten views. This triggers the algorithm to show your video to more individuals. The algorithm is triggered by the speed of the engagements it gets. Content that gets not as much as the like-view rate of 1/10 will stop growing. The uniqueness of Tik Tok is that you do not need to bother with a strong following to become a web sensation. Anybody can record a video, share it on Tik Tok, and begin to get views based on this algorithm. Additionally, what hashtags you use, your location, music choices, and even the absolute first Tik Tok video you like, they would all be able to influence the Tik Tok algorithm.

What makes Tik Tok different from other applications like Instagram and Snapchat is that Tik Tok utilizes artificial intelligence to decide precisely how great your video is. It ranks you on a scale of ten views to tens of millions of views. Adding to this, the higher the level of fulfillment your video gets, the more it gets spread. As your distribution grows, the algorithm takes into account the time that your video needs to continue to grow at the same pace. This means it is a lot easier to go from 10 followers to 100 followers than from 50,000 followers to 100,000 followers.

Complete views have a great weight in the algorithm, it is suggested to keep your videos between 10-15 seconds if you want to become famous online. Tik Tok has many features that can help creativity, like stickers, filters, and music overlays that can catch the attention of the audience.

Tik Tok has legitimately earned its place among the social media application elites.

Brands that can be adaptable and adjust their content and channel to deal with the ever-changing social media scene can reap the benefits. This is some genuine Intel for brands and organizations hoping to get higher engagement with their Tik Tok content and how you can begin to use it for your own benefit.

How to Use Tik Tok's Algorithm to Get Your Content on the "For You" Page

If you are a brand, business, or content creator on Tik Tok, the point is that you want to get more views, likes, and comments on your content. After all, the more eyes on your videos, the higher the opportunity you have to engage your Tik Tok audience and show off your brand. And the key to getting greater engagement on your videos is working with Tik Tok's algorithm to get your content on as many "For You" page as possible. Be that as it may, getting the desired spot on a "For You" page takes something more than adding #fyp to your caption significantly.

To assist you with creating the best content and get more spotlight on the Tik Tok feed there are a few factors that influence Tik Tok's algorithm, from nailing your hashtag strategy to choosing trending songs and sounds, which are parts of the approaches, to hack the Tik Tok algorithm: Factors taken into account by Tik Tok's algorithm include (but are not limited to): Hashtags, Tik Tok captions, use of trending songs and sounds, posting when one's audience is most active, video content and editing and finally location.

While there's no one definitive formula for hacking the algorithm, there are a couple of different factors that could influence video performance and your follower growth as Tik Tok algorithms continually grow, change, and Acquire information from our actions on the application. These factors include consistency, Tik Tok duets, new features, and completion rate.

Tracking Your Tik Tok Analytics and Statistics

Tik Tok is a developing platform that represents a unique opportunity for brands which hope to drive higher engagement on a younger audience.

Although the platform has an enormous user base, one reason brands have been hesitant to add Tik Tok to their marketing was the absence of analytics. With no in-application analytics tool, it was hard for brands to value platform outcomes from the resources they were dispensing. It additionally implied that brands partnering together with influencers couldn't gauge the effectiveness of their collaboration.

Presently with the introduction of Tik Tok's native analytics, joined with Pentos' third-party tool, brands can value the performance of their content on the platform. With analytics finally available, they can have a reliable screen of the platform's outcomes and assess what is the best move to do next.

Obviously, before hopping into the platform, brands must ensure Tik Tok is ideal for their brand. If their ideal content does not include the platform's average user, it probably won't be worth it assigning the resources to the experiment. Beyond driving engagement, it's essential to decide whether the platform will assist them with obtaining users and reach their goals.

Social media is buzzing with Tik Tok's explosive growth, and that is why it is so significant to understand Tik Tok analytics. Track the correct statistics, so you can be able to differentiate hype from reality. If your brand is new to Tik Tok, analytics can remove some guesswork from content strategy. Available insights on Tik Tok pro accounts can give you valuable information about anything, from when you post to what you post. So, brands must realize which Tik Tok statistics they should track, where to find them, and how they can utilize them for their potential benefit.

The fundamental distinction between a Tik Tok pro account and a standard one comes down to Tik Tok analytics. Pro accounts offer analytics, while regular accounts do not. Much like Instagram creator profiles, Tik Tok pro accounts let content creators have insight about audience and performance. From the Tik Tok analytics dashboard, Pro account holders can learn about their followers, track their views and engagement, and do a lot more. A regular Tik Tok account can be changed to a pro account.

Changing to a pro account is simple; start by going to your profile settings and tap the 'manage my account' option. On the following screen, tap switch to a pro account. Next, you are prompted to choose a featured category for your account. The category includes media, personal blogs, entertainment, public figure, education, and more. The last step is to enter a telephone number for your account and afterward enter the code you get through SMS. When you've set up your pro account, go back to the Settings menu, then you will see 'observe an analytics' option. Tap the option button to open your Tik Tok analytics dashboard.

Tik Tok analytics will now start to record data; the dashboard will not show any past data. You will have to wait up to seven days for your account to produce enough data to start showing insights. During this period, it is suggested that you share as much content as possible so you can get deeper insights. Once the analytics begins to give you feedback, you can plunge into your account insights. Similar to all analytics, this data will become more precise and accurate after some time, as you share more content.

Brands should quantify views, engagement (likes, comments, and shares) and reach to evaluate their campaign's success. Tik Tok has likewise started permitting users to include profile links, which means businesses would now be able to direct people to their sites from the application and direct followers to shopping destinations.

Regarding statistics, now the most significant challenge with brands attempting to use influencer marketing and promoting on the application is the difficulty of executing and evaluating campaigns with a group of influencers simultaneously. Gathering data manually can turn into an overwhelming task; however, it's an absolute necessity if the effect of a campaign has to be determined.

Influencer marketing platforms can be useful in this regard, since they automatically gather, analyze, and present data in a relatable manner that bodes well and helps one focus and guide future efforts. While thinking about whether Tik Tok influencer marketing is a fit for your brand, it makes sense to apply guidelines similar to those you would use on other social media platforms.

This Tik Tok statistics is a good sign of brand interest. It gauges the number of individuals who appreciated your video enough to look at your profile or individuals interested in seeing what your brand is up to on the platform. TikTok analytics makes your marketing campaign easier as it analyzes any TikTok profile, hashtags, videos, and songs to understand the platform and grow your business very fast.

There are three main classes that Tik Tok displays within your account dashboard:

1. Profile overview: The profile overview tab is valuable for identifying how well your Tik Tok profile is generally performing. This information includes your total video views, profile views, and follower number.

2. Content insights: The followers' tab in Tik Tok analytics shows a top-line perspective on your audience demographics. You can see the gender split and and the locations of your audience organized by percentage rate. Since Tik Tok has scaled over different nations, you can hope to have audience from all over the world.

3. Follower insights: The Content tab in Tik Tok analytics offers the most extravagant insights. Just like in an "aerial view", you can see the total views on every video post from the previous seven days, showed all together from newest to the oldest.

CHAPTER SIX
Entrepreneurs on Tik Tok

As the utilization of video keeps on ascending in all aspects of life, from entertainment to guidance to news, it turns into a more significant marketing impact. Wyzowl's state of video marketing 2020 reports that the number of businesses using videos as a marketing tool has expanded from 61% in 2016 to 85% projected for 2020. Part of the reason behind the rising speculation is that customers currently watch an average of 16 hours of online video every week, a 52 % expansion since 2018. Despite everything, they still want more.

86% of individuals might want to see more videos from brands, as indicated by

Wyzowl, with 36%wanting more educational/instructive videos and 14% interested in more product demos. In an assessment of how, or where, advertisers plan on using videos, the report found that Youtube, Facebook, and LinkedIn were the top performers; however, 15% intend to invest in TikTok promotions. When asked about their prosperity rates with video over all platforms, 79% of respondents to the Wyzowl study revealed having been productive and successful. On Tik Tok specifically, however, 66%report achievements. Many see Tik Tok as offering unimagined potential, proposing that now, not later is an ideal time to start using it.

A digital trend report revealed that out of 11 minutes spent on a cell phone, 10 minutes are on an application. That implies the opportunity is there to create brand awareness. Tik Tok may appear just like another app for kids, but if its growth is compared to that of other social platforms, it turns out that Instagram needed six years.

It took some time, but Tik Tok finally introduced ads on the platform. A worldwide overview by Global Web Index found that 52% of Tik Tok users internationally would purchase an item just to be a part of the community. Furthermore, 61% will, in general, purchase advertised products. The application offers exact targeting, so you can ensure that your advertisements are reaching the specific users who would be keen on what you have to offer.

Tik Tok offers four unique types of advertisements. There is in-feed native content; this kind of ad is like Snapchat or Instagram story advertisements and supports different features like website clicks or application downloads. You can gauge the campaign's success through tracking clicks, impressions, click-through rate (CTR), video views, and engagement.

Brand takeovers are those that let brands take over Tik Tok for the day. A brand takeover promotion springs up when somebody opens Tik Tok. They can create pictures, GIFs, and videos with embedded links to landing pages or hashtag challenges. Tik Tok just permits one advertiser for this format per day and ensures five million daily impressions.

There are branded lenses, which resemble the Snapchat 2D and 3D lenses for faces and photographs. As indicated by Tik Tok, 64% of its users have attempted face filters and lenses.

Lastly, there are hashtag challenges; rather than trying to make a hashtag challenge famous online, you can use promoted hashtags to get higher engagement.

TikTok is here, and it doesn't appear to be going anywhere. If you want your business to grow and have success, becoming acquainted with Tik Tok is a good first step. It is a video-sharing platform that rose out of relative obscurity to become one of the leading social companies globally, and one of the most business-friendly for entrepreneurs who know how to make it work.

Tik Tok is specially crafted for personal-brand building, and numerous entrepreneurs are utilizing it in just that way. This is an ideal opportunity to get acquainted with Tik Tok; Tik Tok is a social media platform that gives content, entertainment, and engagement for most millennials. The platform supports just a video format of 15 to 60 seconds to catch users' short attention span.

Tik Tok is winning on social media platforms since it is not difficult to use, it is very creative, and has a user-friendly algorithm. These characteristics put together are a 100% reliable formula for

for taking over Instagram and Facebook. Where Tik Tok stands out is in producing brand awareness and engagement. Users that can combine engaging or useful content in a 15-or 60-second video clip can observe practically immediate results. And the use of Tik Tok for creating videos for advertisements and advancement is cost-friendly as most videos cost nothing; all the cutting and editing are in-app features, so it doesn't require any special tool or editing software.

Businesses ready to be funny and engaging, or to make fun of themselves, can witness a fast growth on TikTok. Right now, this seems to be one of the brands' advertising secret.

Dos and Don'ts for Entrepreneurs on TikTok

Anyone who wants to build a marketing campaign on TikTok should know the following do's and don'ts:

1. Keep your videos light and fun: Tik Tok is an opportunity to show a more creative and entertaining side of your brand. While making videos for advertisements or advancement, such videos should be made simple and Relatable for your audience.

2. Be spontaneous: Content that is hilarious, real life, and casual plays the best; videos that jump directly to the point and are around 15 seconds long are preferred.

3. Use music: Music is a significant part of Tik Tok and can be used deliberately to make videos all the more fascinating and engaging.

4. Do proper formatting for the platform: When shooting videos, ensure that they are vertical and not horizontal.

5. Start a challenge: Start campaigns that challenge users to make and share Tik Tok videos related to the challenge, use the hashtag #Hashtag Challenge, and tag three of their friends to challenge them and spread your campaign.

6. Respond to other brand challenges: In addition, to starting your brand challenge, take an interest in challenges set up by other businesses.

7. Mimic content that is trending: As a brand, you must intently monitor what's trending on a daily basis to rapidly reproduce the content that will spread your products and services to potential users.

8. Collaborate with influencers and partners: Brands can engage or collaborate with influencers on Tik Tok; Tik Tok influencer has built an army that can enhance engagement and awareness towards your brand rapidly.

9. Keep good customer relationships: Customers should be treated like kings, as their complaints are promptly treated.

10. Do not make a hard-sell advertisement: If your business has a product, the best kind of content possible is one that showcases your product, but do not feel just like a simple ad.

CHAPTER SEVEN

Understanding Hashtags and Hashtag Challenges

Starting a business could be a confusing experience. You might not know which direction you want to give to your business. Several entrepreneur which are now successful had that experience, too.

Creating hashtags is like creating a brand. You get to see this as you Dive in this new chapter of your life. Hashtags also help you see competitors, as well as your visibility to them. In this chapter, we will be going through the history of hashtags and its relevance in increasing one's influence on Tik Tok.

History of Hashtags

Chris Messina, is one whose name cannot be forgotten when it comes to how hashtags started. Hashtag was seen as a nerdy thing on twitter. It enables the user to apply dynamic, and user-generated metadata tag. It could be made in the form of letters, digits, and underscores. So, anyone who looks for a particular word or tag sees all posts in which the tags appear.

Chris Messina's first use of the hashtag was in a 2007 tweet. Although Twitter did not adopt it according to Messina's suggestion, it became a common feature for many people. Many other social platforms like Facebook, Instagram, YouTube, Reddit, and even Tik Tok are not left out from its use. Gen Z, millennials, influencers, celebrities, and even entrepreneurs commonly use these tags.

"Hashtag," due to its widespread use, was added to the Oxford English Dictionary as of 2014. Personalities use hashtags to promote their corporate or personal Twitter accounts and receive mentions and replies to posts. To trend hashtags, it is often encouraged to use it not just on twitter but also on other search engines.

Political protests and campaigns like the #blacklivesmatter movement or the #OccupyWallStreet have been organized thanks to hashtags. These went viral since any hashtag, if promoted by enough people, can trend and become famous.

Why hashtags?

It is a linking medium; it forms a community of thoughts, words, actions, and characters. It connects people and ideas, which is the goal of most social media platforms; An entrepreneur's proper use of hashtags will determine, to a large extent, how successful he/she is on the internet.

How hashtags should be used?

Use popular tags

Using trending hashtags on a post can increase the visibility of your post on Tik Tok. One can find trending tags by being active on social media. Popular tags could build campaigns. Popular videos on Tik Tok have tags attached to them. Find out what they are and use them at the right time. The timing is also a factor involved in the success of the tag. When you use a tag that trended in 2014, there will be very little importance unless there is a current campaign similar to that.

It is also possible to create one that will be trending. Experts suggest using one alongside a trending tag. So, when a lot of individuals see the posts according to their popularity, they see that tag you have just created too.

As an entrepreneur, another advice is not to be too eager to use popular hashtags that do not go with your niche. Popular hashtags meet a broader audience, but niche hashtags are more specific and will reach people who are more likely to engage with your post. Niche hashtags, therefore, bring you further in the sales funnel.

Use specific brand tags.

This depends on what kind of product or service you are offering on Tik Tok. Since personalities "trend" tags, many big brands do this too. If these tags are relevant to your product, then go ahead. The "Discover" page on Tik Tok is an excellent place to search for the right trending tags. Whether they are industry-related, location tags, or modifies #forsale hashtags, it all goes.

Keep it simple

Whatever new hashtag you tend to create for your brand, it shouldn't be too long or complicated. The rule here is relevance (as we've been saying) and specificity. It should also not be too generic. Recently, Instagram banned some too generic hashtags like #photography #iphoneography #sexy #popular and many more. "A hashtag is blocked because it returns inappropriate or pornographic results that exceed a certain threshold," says Ksenia Zaharova in her book, "How to Sell on Instagram." It is also wise to apply these rules on Tik Tok.

Do not overuse them

Just because hashtags on Tik Tok are fresh, unlike the ones on Instagram or Twitter, this does not mean they should be overused. Tik Tok limits the caption to be just 100 characters, therefore maximize hashtags, but do not overuse them. Avoid creating a post with more than 30 hashtags. It just displays you as a hungry person, hunting for popularity at all costs. It somehow created distrust in the minds of your fans and others who will see that video.

The Relevance of self-created hashtags to Entrepreneurs

Website owners know the importance of Search Engine Optimization (SEO) to online marketing. That same importance can quantify the relevance of hashtags on social media platforms like Tik Tok. Every user on Tik Tok can create their hashtags, whether they are new to the platform or have been there for a while. Using other users' hashtags helps increase one's content reach, so do self-created hashtags apply to a specific niche?

When doing a particular marketing campaign, it is wise to create a hashtag for all content created for the campaign. This also helps to keep track and easily find anything related to the campaign.

If a new project is coming, it is great to create a hashtag for that and make people anticipate the campaign by creating content around it and giving people sneak peeks to fuel their curiosity. Many influential people use it to announce the launch of a new start-up or a new idea and create a buzz about the project.

Customers can also use the hashtag created for a specific product when they buy or review the product. This will increase the popularity of hashtags. This is one of the two ways to get free and quality user-generated content.

The last but not the least benefit is that the hashtag challenge could also increase the popularity of the brand on other social platforms just like the #icebucket or the #pepsicanbalance challenge that went all over social media.

Some popular hashtags

Some of the popular hashtags on Tik Tok as of June 2020 are;

#blacklivesmatter

#dadsoftiktok

#yogaglow

#juneteenth

#beyourselfchallenge

#fyp

#thanksdad

The Hashtag Challenge

This is an indirect method to drag fans and engage other users on Tik Tok. From Guess to Jimmy Fallon, to Chipotle, it has rapidly increased online engagement and brand impact. The idea behind this is that people create content that increases their brand's impact and brings potential benefits in the long run. On Tik Tok, these challenges are spearheading enormous engagement on the platform. Users like these challenges because they are dynamic, and each user can interpret the challenge in their own way. Brands are also free to create their own challenge rules, custom sounds and effects, and anything else about the challenge.

However, these challenges could be expensive for start-ups. It is advisable to encourage the audience to follow these challenges with ads and brand takeovers to drive awareness on the challenge. These challenges can then be linked to different landing pages to generate leads for the brand.

Chipotle started a #Guacdance challenge, on The National Avocado Day, which required users to make videos of dance moves dedicated to Guacamole. They got 900 million+ views and tremendously increased sales.

Jimmy Fallon, who was new on Tik Tok at the time, started a collaborated challenge, called #tumbleweedchallenge and had around 30 million views.

Another popular hashtag challenge is the #inmydenim challenge by Guess, a company that markets jeans. Users had to show how they wear their products. This resulted in more than 40 million views.

Tips to Understand when to create your hashtag challenges

Ask yourself the following questions when creating a branded hashtag.

- What do you want to be the result of your hashtags: popularity, or engagement?

- What is your niche?

This is an example of a demographic to engage for a particular hashtag. Remember, as discussed in previous chapters, they should be broad, yet specific. Other tips are:

- Follow current trends or people that are doing what you would like to do on Tik Tok?

- Think solely about your product, but make people see that it can give balance to their personality and class.

- Use effects and animation to make it fun, engaging, and create something unique for your brand.

- Create rules and make the users follow them.

- Give users the freedom to be dynamic with whatever content they are creating for the challenge.

- Create social currency.

- Use popular memes.

- Select a name that fits the hashtag challenge. People can easily relate to it and remember it.

- The effective use of sounds should also not be neglected.

It is best to study popular hashtags challenges all over social media, know what made them go viral, and try to implement relevant lessons learned to suit your needs. I hope you will use these tools, "Hashtags" and generate mind-blowing leads.

CHAPTER EIGHT

Running an Influencer Marketing Campaign

One of the most important criteria for online marketing (and any marketing) is that you reach the kind of people you think will become your customers. Influencer marketing means you have to do one step back and focus on the people who are liked by your target customers and are able to influence their behavior. If you sell to a young audience, you might consider working on Tik Tok with influencers.

When most people think of influencers and marketing, they usually think about traditional social media channels:

Facebook, Instagram, and Twitter. Influencer marketing, however, started long before Instagram became the place for ambassadors for celebrity brands.

Who is an influencer?

An influencer is an individual or group with personal authority, attitude, expertise, or relationships which affect others' purchasing decisions. An influencer can be a known figure in a particular industry, topic area, or niche that has gained a following. The main characteristic of influencers is that either through expertise or experience, they have built a relationship with their audience. Examples of people we consider influencers are famous figures, gamers, bloggers, industry experts, and social media influencers.

Tik Tok Influencers

Social media influencers (such as Tik Tok) have built a reputation for their knowledge and expertise on a particular subject matter. They make they make posts on their preferred social media channel on a regular basis and generate substantial follow-ups from enthusiastic, engaged people who pay close attention to their videos.

You may also describe social media influencer as someone who, thanks to his/her authority or relationship with target customers, may affect the individual's purchases. The definition of social media influencer goes beyond the number of followers that can attract such people to a social media network or website. The ability to build engagement with the core audience on the street is crucial for a brand.

Marketing campaigns

Marketing campaigns promote products via various media, such as e-television, radio, print, and online platforms. Campaigns are not exclusively advertising-based and may include demonstrations, video conferencing, and other interactive techniques. Companies operating in highly competitive markets and franchises should conduct regular marketing campaigns and commit considerable resources to these campaigns.

Tik Tok's Marketing Campaigns

Tik Tok's marketing ecosystem is new, but brands jump into the advertisement potential of this app. Below are a couple of different ways to incorporate Tik Tok marketing.

1. IN-FEED ADS

2. BRAND TAKEOVER ADS

3. TIK TOK HASHTAG CHALLENGE ADS

4. TIK TOK SHOPPABLE ADS: THE 'HASHTAG CHALLENGE PLUS'

5. BRANDED TIK TOK STICKERS

6. TIK TOK INFLUENCER MARKETING ADS

Influencer Marketing Campaigns

Influencer marketing is a form of social media marketing involving endorsements and placement of products from influencers, individuals, and organizations that have a supposed level of knowledge or social influence in their field. Influencer content can be framed as testimonial advertising; influencers play the role of a potential buyer, or third parties may be involved.

As with all influencer marketing, partnering with influencer's whose followers suit your target audience is crucial to success on Tik Tok. Therefore you need to appeal to Tik Tok demographic for influencer marketing to be successful for you on Tik Tok.

How to go about an influencer marketing campaign

The most effective form of marketing on Tik Tok is influencer marketing. You don't suffer from ads' negative implications, and you don't have to worry about building the right audience as you do on your company account with native videos. You just need to collaborate with the right influencer to come up with an innovative approach that will help them pique their audience's interest in building interest in your brand and product.

How to Build a Tik Tok Influencer Marketing Strategy

Marketers should follow these steps in order to develop an impacting marketing strategy for Tik Tok influencer:

1. Understand Tik Tok Platform

If Tik Tok is unchartered territory, do not immerse yourself without research to determine if your brand is ready to launch a campaign. If you are reading this guide, you are learning if Tik Tok is a good platform for your brand or not. Test new ways to reach your target audience or consider working with a reputable marketing agency, such as Mediakix, who knows the platform and has established relationships with Tik Tok creators.

2. Determine Campaign Goals for Tik Tok.

Consider what your ultimate aim is for the campaign of your brand — is it pushing UGC or motivating users to use your app? Consider the goals, and know which KPIs you will use to calculate the effectiveness of the campaign. Clearly defined objectives enable you to measure your campaign's ROI and overall strategy.

3. Research & Vet influencer Tik Tok.

The Tik Tok creators you want to partner with ought to be carefully researched. Do they have a proven track record of high-quality content? Do they receive real commitment? Is their audience attuned to yours? Do their preferences and values suit your brands authentically? Do not partner with an influencer based solely on vanity metrics (e.g., followers) on Tik Tok but do some effort to understand if they fit your goals.

4. Let Tik Tok Express Creativity

With the newness of Tik Tok, brands might be tempted to exert too much creative control over what is being published. Trust the platform creators who have established authenticity in their space. Refrain from taking away their creative spark and let influencers to get input — this will also go a long way in the growth of a long-term relationship with the influencer.

5. Measure the results of the Tik Tok campaign.

It goes without saying, but it is pointless to conduct a campaign without knowing how to evaluate its success. Know general performance benchmarks to continuously test and optimize your marketing strategy for Tik Tok influencers. If your goal is brand impact, see how many views the collaboration earns, how much engagement the post generates.

6. Ensuring sponsorships for Tik Tok influencers and FTC-compliant.

Brands should check if their Tik Tok influencers have serve for other brands on other social media platforms. Should know that FTC violations can be very expensive for a brand. Ensure that influencer of Tik Tok use # ad and comply with FTC guidelines to avoid getting into a legal mess.

7. Seek other advertisement types on Tik Tok.

Building a strong marketing strategy for Tik Tok influencers can be a lucrative endeavor for your brand. Combine it with other Tik Tok advertising tactics, so to get the most out of the platform. This will boost the presence of your brand and it will strengthen your overall marketing efforts at Tik Tok.

How to find Tik Tok influencers

To launch a marketing campaign that impacts on Tik Tok, you will need to find reputable Tik Tok influencers to partner with. As in every marketing strategy for influencers, marketers must exert their best judgment when choosing influencers to represent their brand. Failing in examining and assessing influencers puts brands at risk of failing the overall marketing campaign on Tik Tok.

Brands should also be familiar with what is essential to influencers in a brand partnership. See the five tips about how to find influencers for Tik Tok to better prepare your brand for a successful Tik Tok marketing influencer campaign:

1. Know your audience.

2. Do Google Organic Search.

3. Check Related, Trending Hashtags on 'Discover Page' by Tik Tok.

4. Identify existing content sponsored by influencers on Tik Tok.

5. Cross-check known influencers on other social networks.

Benefits of running an influencer marketing campaign

Here are six significant advantages of using influencer marketing to strengthen your social strategy.

1. Builds confidence fast

The influencers have established relationships with their followers. Plus, they have confidence with their audience and they can boast a good reputation with them.

People respect their content and recommendations. By sharing the content of an influencer, you will get their attention soon and and they will start sharing yours, putting your message before an active audience.

2. Improves awareness towards the brand

As mentioned above, influencer marketing can significantly increase your online reach and positioning. Social users can learn more about your brand, your background, who you are, and the products you offer. The secret to optimizing influencer strategy is to ensure that you also have meaningful content that adds value to both sides of their social media activity.

3. Enriches your approach on the web

Sharing influencer content will help you fill the holes on your posting schedule. It works well in case you run out of ideas about the material to post or when you need some quality material to shar on your social media.

4 Reaches the target market effectively

This is one of the most important tips. Your content is placed in front of social users who are already interested in your niche through relevant influencers. You don't have to spend extra money on testing and finding your audience. The influencer has filtered and fostered this audience on social media already.

5. Provides the audience with tremendous value

The centerpiece of inbound marketing is to deliver content that solves problems, educates, and inspires your intended public. This concept is embraced by influencer marketing, as influencers are already in tune with the needs of the people they serve. In turn, you can easily leverage their content to give your audience value.

6. Builds Partnerships

Connecting and becoming engaged with an influencer may be the beginning of a great relationship. You never know where those connections could end when you are in it for the long-haul. There could be future joint-ventures, live activities, and other partnerships at stake.

Benefits of working with an influencer

Influencers are valuable because they offer credibility to a growing company which need it. Their peers' recommendations influence 70 percent of millennials. Influencers provide a point of connection between companies and the target market. Working with someone who influences:

1. Increases brand impact: Gain access to a global audience with your influencer. This market is already engaged and is waiting for appropriate content.

2. Builds trust: Consumers already trust the opinions of those influencers they are following. Influencers instantaneously boost your brand's credibility.

3. Improves customer relationships: Strengthen customer relationships through intimate customer relationships.

4. Improves the brand: The definite link that influencers have with consumers alone creates a "halo impact" that enhances the business at the consumer's eyes.

5. **Improves SEO:** Working with influencer's offers link-building opportunities. More links lead to better search rankings

Now that you are aware of the pros and cons of marketing with Tik Tok influencers, it is time to build your campaign. Whether you are doing influencer marketing for the first time on Tik Tok or you are trying to optimize your strategy, you can partner with an experienced marketing agency to launch an impacting campaign with a Tik Tok influencer.

Influencer marketing can be incredibly beneficial for startup brands or those who have struggled to gain grip in their marketing on social media. With a strong understanding of how influencer marketing can drive your online goals, you can commit to quickly launch your first campaign to see those results in your company.

CHAPTER NINE

Uncertainties and Certainties of Social Media As Regards To Business

For months now, advertisers have used Tik Tok to promote their companies. For others, social media marketing can be a fantastic way to work. It sounds incredible, right? It is — but those case studies are becoming quite challenging to find. These days, many marketers find their organic growth stagnating from social media. Although 77 percent of marketers Use at least one social media platform for marketing purposes, less than half (48%) say that they see ROI from this strategy.

In this chapter, the certainties and uncertainties of Tik Tok regarding business will be extensively discussed. Also, it is essential not to forget that there are always two sides of the coin, as far as ROI are concerned, half of the chances is to have good results from this strategy

A business is defined as an enterprise or organization engaged in commercial, industrial, or professional activities. Businesses may be for-profit corporations, or they may be non-profit organizations that work to fulfill a charitable mission or a social cause.

The general concept is when an individual or company profits in return for money by supplying products or services. But profit can include other value items, such as credit and exchange items and services instead of money.

Business in the 21st century regarding Internet presence

The world wide web has revolutionized and changed the way we do business. The Internet has changed and influenced every aspect of our society. It also affected the business. The Internet has changed the rules of the play. It has put everyone in connection and now anyone can be an entrepreneur if he/she has a little bit of creativity.

It has never been easier to start a business. All you need, except of course a profitable idea, is some hosting money, and that is all about it. You can do everything else, from getting content up on the website and creating the logo, promoting it on social media. That is why there have never been more companies, and the potential to make money has never been this high in past centuries.

Social media platforms and business

Today, tons of social media platforms are available to marketers, and they play a significant role in your success in social media marketing. Factors such as your industry, your audience and your brand can all influence the social network that you are using.

Social media marketing is a powerful tool to reach prospects and customers for businesses of all sizes. Your customers already interact with brands through social media, and if you don't speak to your audience directly through social platforms, you are missing out! Great social media marketing can bring remarkable success to your business, creating dedicated brand advocates and even driving leads and sales.

Tik Tok and business

Tik Tok app has been downloaded more than 750 million times in the past 12 months, outpacing last year's Facebook, Instagram, Twitter, and Snapchat rivals.

By using Tik Tok correctly, you can attract a huge audience to your company or product. In fact, according to Influencer Marketing Hub, Tik Tok has 800 million active users worldwide, and it was Apple's most downloaded app.

If your business has a young target audience, Tik Tok users' largest demographic is between 16 and 24 years of age. Tik Tok is the perfect place to grab their attention. Tik Tok has evolved from a video-creation app designed solely for users to express their creativity into a marketing and advertising haven since its birth in 2018. Brands have created accounts on the platform over the last 12 months to explore and engage with consumers.

Tik Tok's allure to enterprises is the sheer number of active users on the platform. How the algorithm works exactly is still unclear, but it seems much easier for your video content to go viral on Tik Tok than on other social media platforms.

How to maximize Tik Tok as an entrepreneur

1. Create fun content

One of the easiest ways to promote your business on Tik Tok as an entrepreneur is by creating your content. You can show off your products with a fun video demonstration and a nice song. Make it simple. A simple video that shows off your products will be seen as more authentic than if your business tries to create memes with the goal to make them go viral.

2. Create a hashtag challenge

Creating a lively hashtag challenge enhances user interaction and engagement and promotes your business. You can encourage Tik Tok users to create or reproduce content and include your brand's hashtag in it.

3. Work with Tik Tok influencers

You can partner with Tik Tok influencers to run marketing campaigns. Influencers have varying numbers of followers, therefore, varying degrees of influencers. Be sure that the influencer's audience is similar to your target audience. Identify online tools that will enable you to look for users' bios, look for other brands' mention, and locate commonly used expressions among an influencer's audience.

4. Maximize your influences

When you have worked on increasing your followers, make sure you maximize your influence over them. Make sure you are not just posting content for the sake of views alone. Make sure they are buying your product. Let your followers transform into customers.

Uncertainties of social media (Tik Tok) as it regards to business

With this understanding, it is best to note that Tik Tok has specific uncertainties in its relation to business.

1. Poor use of analytical techniques that do not require high precision.

Data Analysis, an understanding of the network, is one of the most important business aspects of a social networking site. Simply put: you cannot monetize what you do not understand.

Simple statistic models are often more reliable than more detailed models for dealing with highly complex situations. This is particularly good advice for marketers, who may be used with two or more decimal places to see awareness and preference data. The problem with dealing with social networks and other dynamic structures is that a simplistic model is more likely to match well with past data but fails to predict the future. A more basic model is less likely to fit past data but more likely to anticipate different future scenarios.

2. Lack of Multi-Outcome Preparation.

It is more probable to have success if you bet on more options, rather than on few specific ones. Place lots of huge bets on a range of options.

3. Not finding and not relying on predictable situational elements.

4. Lack of Emphasis on Inputs assessment of initiatives.

Randomness will scatter even the best efforts to produce results, so the quality of the decision to undertake it may not be considered when assessing the success of an initiative. Don't rely solely on the project's actual outcome (bad or good), but take into account the quality of the process that went into it.

5. It requires human power to stay agile and strive to react quickly.

As soon as they happen, there is no substitute for perception, listening, and detecting events. As an organization, you are asked to focus on "sense and respond," and act quickly and decisively. As a rule, have a precise principle, a strong social media policy but generic enough to be flexible, while keeping that the actual results may vary.

In the end, you have to prepare for failure, success, and everything in between. But as long as others find you trustworthy, you will never be alone. Focus on doing the right thing, and your customers, staff, and other stakeholders will all be interested in seeing your business grow.

Some statistics

A quick look at these statistics reveals social media's potential for business. It is also important to remember that most of the figures on the outcomes and the estimates are closer to 50%, which resonates with the complexities of social media as they relate to the company. The statistics are below:

Social Media for Business:

53% of small enterprises use social media.

53% of active users of social media follow a brand.

Sales increased by 43% of marketers due to social campaigns.

Customer relations and social media:

Social media users who experienced poor service will tell their experience to an average of 53 people. Men and women who are not social media user will tell to 17 people.

20% of social media users would buy on a social media site.

50% of small business owners reported receiving new clients via social media activities.

47% of consumers are somewhat likely to buy online from a brand they are following.

The other side of the coin

A lot has been understood, but will one allow even a small company to go global without enormous investments? For example, Brand24 is a business that employs less than 50 employees, but acquired clients in more than 35 countries worldwide, by merely optimizing social networking over the years. How do you leverage these platforms within your company? What is constant about social networking?

1. It allows for more personal relationships (Show Authenticity).

Social networking is a twofold platform where you can develop a relationship with your present and future customers. Social media helps humanize a brand and create real group relationships.

2. It encourages entrepreneurship more effectively.

According to a study, 78 percent of small businesses attract new customers through social media. Thanks to the advanced targeting and remarketing options, you can send your message to the audience that is more likely to be interested in your products and services. Tik Tok's paid ads are relatively cheap, cheap and, if you have a well knitted web on the social platform, one's efforts will pay off.

3. It offers useful insights into consumers and companies.

Users inquire, suggest, but post feedback as well. They are the best source of information about possible product developments. Those who use your service or product know best what can be improved to fit their needs. The feedback is gold to get answers about the preferences and behavior of your customers.

4. It sparks loyalty.

According to a study by Texas Tech University, brands actively participating in social media interactions continue to experience improved brand loyalty. When the business is active on social networking platforms, you become more open and credible to the eyes of consumers and potential customer.

Other verified reasons which have stood the test of time remains:

1. It improves brand awareness.

2. It remains cost-effective.

3. It amplifies brand authority.

4. It increases traffic.

5. It enhances SEO rankings.

Social media is the right tool for all this. If you can take advantage of its possibilities, your company can indeed prosper from it. You can achieve marketing goals with fewer resources with a good strategy, some creativity, and additional tools.

Despite all that has been said, Tik Tok remains a vital tool for business in this century and cannot be overruled. According to a McKinley Global Institute report, over the past five years, the Internet largely accounted for 21 percent of GDP growth in mature economies. The future is even brighter, as the same report concludes: "We are still in the early stages of transformation, the internet will unleash and the opportunities it will foster."

When it comes to the economy and business growth, we also have to enjoy the worldwide network's full benefits. Our culture is changing rapidly, and anyone who fails in adapting will have to face the consequences of it. If you are not applying this valuable advice, you will miss an incredible marketing opportunity because it makes it easy and efficient to spread the word about your product and mission.

CONCLUSION

There is no doubt that Tik Tok is here to stay. Tik Tok has its unique features although it shares some aesthetic and functional similarity with Snapchat and Instagram. Brands who have effectively tuned to Tik Tok early on have received tremendous brand awareness benefits, often with very little investment.

Brands must position themselves as a creative force to be recognized by a new, global and young audience. This book has presented the various benefits of using Tik Tok as an entrepreneur. It has also explained how to maximize influencers on Tik Tok and run marketing ads in order to reach a wider audience.

Use the tips on how to promote your business on Tik Tok that you found in this book and you will be awed by the sudden, positive turnaround that business will have.

If you want to learn more, get the best comprehensive course here:

[QR code: SCAN ME]

(affiliate link)

Stay up to date on the author's upcoming publications, write to:
robertkasey70@gmail.com

Made in the USA
Middletown, DE
31 July 2021